DRAB LIL, A GYPSY'S MEDICINE BOOK
by Clarissa Simmens
(aka Viata Maya Suharliavi)

A Treatise on the Drom Ek Romani, Tarot and Numerology

Cover art by Karen S. Bruton
"Nantyllan Morning"
copyright 2013

Dedicated to

My *Drabarni* Ancestors:

Estana, Haika, Rae-Rae and Sonja

My Medicine Book

Will it take a century to be read
Just like the Book of Talismans I found?
A hundred years lying like the undead
Surfacing in the dark of night, unbound?

Or will it wait upon a shelf somewhere?
Or molder on the web's ancient server?
Discovered by a person who will care,
Or public domain miners with fervor?

The Cemetery of Forgotten Books
As created by Carlos R. Zafon
Is modernized in Kindles and in Nooks
And would serve as the perfect stepping stone.

So here is my book for posterity
Please try to read it with sincerity!

TABLE OF CONTENTS

First Page Disclaimer
(What this book IS NOT about)

Drab, in Romanes, means herb and fortunetelling. A *drabarni* is one who can heal with herbs and advise by using cards, tea leaves, dreams and the lines on the palm of the hand. Let's change the word *fortunetelling* because no future is engraved into gold and our past will determine our actions for the future. It is more a holistic way of looking at another's life and prescribing—through the use of herbs and advice—how to cope with life.

This book is one Romani's (Gypsy) *grimoire*, a family compendium about moving along our path in life with a minimum amount of stress. It is not meant to be a guide but it is a slice of life that I hope you will learn from and enjoy.

I am glad you can look inside this book before you buy it and I will tell you immediately what this book is NOT:

--I will not teach you how to read cards but I will encourage you to make your own by using your personal symbols, pictures (stick people ok), interpretations and position in the *drom* or path or way.

--I will not list herbs and their curative powers or tell you how to physically heal anyone. I consider myself a healer of the soul, not a physical healer, because I do not have the talent to deal with a physical body but I can listen carefully to people and give my opinion by the use of the *Drom Ek Romani.*

--I will not list references but I will use the words "I don't know" many times because the Roma and Sinti had an oral tradition, not a written one, so this knowledge was passed down through the centuries by mouth. Most importantly, and the reason why I call it the Drom EK Romani (ek means one) is because I believe each generation made certain symbols our own through observation, technology and necessity and each interpretation was passed on to our descendants. The original meanings have been subtly altered as we progressed through the centuries. So if, like me, one is an

11

Eastern European Kalderash and Sinti, then the slave mentality has shaped my thoughts because Roma (Gypsies) were enslaved from the middle ages until the 1800s and many of us are part European because of the DNA forced upon the female slaves. In my family, the non-Gypsy part has manifested in light skin and light eyes but has not diluted our love of freedom.

So why write this book when I don't know certain things? I know it is something I must do, must record. Consider it my *sunengo lil* (book of dreaming) or *drukerdo lil* (fortunetelling book) or *farmechi ramomate (spell diary)*. Consider it my gift to you...

INTRODUCTION
(What this book IS about)

In these pages you will find a commentary, based on my life's path, depicted on my own Drom Ek Romani that includes the bits of culture that my *phuri dai* (grandmother) taught me. The wooden disks or cards are my own personal cards and interpretations that I have devised in the hope of keeping the precious culture alive. Drom means "way" or "road" and Romani is the correct word for Gypsy. So this is the "Way of the Romani people." Of course, as my grandmother would say, it is the "way of (one) Gypsy," and that is me.

You will notice that the commentary is written in 22 chapters, each one with the title of the 22 cards of the Drom Romani. I have tried to show how life often follows each little path as we spiral through it.
The number 22 is very karmic and is used in the tarot as well as the Drom. I was told that we, the Roma, wrote the tarot, so to speak, well before it appeared in Fifteenth Century Italy as originally believed. Some symbols are gathered from the lore absorbed from my grandmother who taught me to read cards, tea leaves, and interpret dreams, and from my father who taught me many mystical things. Some symbols are personal, some are those I've come across in my years of research.

Cards have always been a tactile thrill, to me. I can feel the power in every deck: the story that is waiting, as if from a book that I am about to read for the first time. I cannot play solitaire or any card game (whether I'm using a deck bought at the supermarket or a fancy one or even a computer deck) without seeing a story; each court card tells me something as does each pip.

When I was about eight, my grandmother drew symbols on small pieces of wood that I have reproduced. She gave me the first five and instructed me to observe life as I grew older and add my own. They could be altered but she hoped I would not commit them to paper (or wood) until I was sure. Although I've been enamored of the tarot most of my life, I discovered that in my mid fifties, the markers and pens found their way to the blank cards I bought and my Drom Ek Romani was completed, all 22 of them.

One of the things that troubled me was the use of the number 22 for Major Arcana and our own Drom Romani. We know from all the scholarly books written about the tarot that the kabbalah is the basis for tarot because there are 22 alphabet letters in Hebrew. So what does that have to do with Gypsies who emigrated from India (based on the language similarity to Sanskrit)? If you have a scholarly bent toward studying numerology that is entwined with the tarot, it would also be advantageous to study Vedic Numerology based on the oldest scriptures of Hinduism: the Vedas. They also believe that the number 22 is highly spiritual, involving the purification of mind and soul. The number 22 is never added together to be 4 and the number 11 is also karmic and never added together to be 2.

We Gypsies traveled, did not have a homeland, and were unable or unwilling to put down roots. So everything was kept simple. I still make dinners where I put the pot of goulash or soup on the table with bowls and spoons and tell all to help themselves, including going into my refrigerator for anything needed. This is my metaphor for not spoon-feeding you. With internet sources such as Wikipedia and Google and overloads of information, it is almost like I am saying, "Help yourself. Here's the pot of soup, you do the rest. My sustenance is your sustenance and I'm here to start you on your path..."

There are websites that will help you determine your special numbers. You can add up your month, day and year of birth to get your Life Path number. Or you can look at the alphabet equivalent to numbers based on your full name

Note: both of mine (full birthday and full name) came out to 5 and while the description of a 5 person is definitely me, I do not vibrate to the actual number 5. I always liked the number 4 since I was a little girl. The vibration is important because like the word Om, numbers have their own vibrations that harmonize in our lives. I will say, in keeping with the "keep it simple" motto, that to me, the most important number is the day we were born. I was born on the 15th so 15 is my number, as is 6 (1+5 = 6). I do not use the letters of my name because I feel that my native language, English, is not the same as Sanskrit or Hindi or Kabbalah Hebrew, so why would one's name, in English, have any meaning in numerology? That's just my personal preference.

Still another note on reading your path whether using cards or wooden disks or runes: Throughout my life I felt that the hand vibrations aided the selection of the symbols by shuffling cards or picking wooden disks out of a bag. At the end of the 1990's, when the internet became a way of life, I discovered a random number generator site. The numbers 1 to 100 were—um—randomly generated and since the author had 5 columns, I would choose the top 5 in the row. The first would represent Earth (security and personal material well-being—Pentacles). The second would be Water (emotions—Cups). The third would be Air (mental—Swords). The fourth would be Fire (spirituality—Wands). And the fifth would represent an overall summary. I eventually found the vibrations to travel from the mouse to my hand and every reading I've done for myself and most others has proven that we can use modern technology to read the page of our path when we need to know it.

So although I strongly encourage you to develop your own symbols and draw your own deck, a computer or cell phone with internet capability is just as good once you have memorized the symbols and their interpretations from your 22 way-stations along your path: the cards.

The Minor Arcana is very useful when details are needed. I have noticed that the older one gets, the less detail is needed. When we are young we have so many friends, family, choices that need to be included. The best book I've read is Muriel Hasbrouck's *Tarot and Astrology: The Pursuit of Destiny*. In it she breaks down the year into 10-day cycles and assigns a Minor Arcana card to each Astrological sign. My birthday is April 15 and so I am Aries and Wands. In her system, Hasbrouck has assigned 10 days to the Four of Wands, that haven of refuge, the house. This is a whole other facet of the personality and I feel it is a very important book for tarot readers. Remember, once you know people's characters, you will be able to better see what path they are spiraling on and whether anything needs to be adjusted in their lives.

So I have had a confusing life. Both families hid the fact of our being Gypsies in the interest of assimilating into American culture. Yet my grandmother and mother kept alive our hidden culture. Since we are only 75% Romani because of slavery, many Roma would not accept us as part of their *vitsa* (nation) and *Gadje*, non-Roma, would just think of us as Gypsies. Being first generation American, it was difficult for me to know myself. But I've learned. My life has been like a palimpsest and so at

15

times I have had to gently erase what has been written over the real hidden manuscript to find the original. This is one of the results.

Yet a third note: any commentary on the tarot will be based on my favorite deck by Rider-Waite.(RWS: adds the all-important artist, Pamela Coleman Smith, to Rider and Waite). Their interpretations are supposedly from ancient times, according to the Golden Dawn. Maybe. I don't know. I do know that they claim the Egyptians began the tarot, and that the word Gypsy comes from Egyptian, so fill in the blanks...

"Figure out the rhythm of life and live in harmony with it"--Lao Tzu, Tao Te Ching

Suggestions for Advising Others

I have always looked at the person who is questioning their future, not the so-called fortune or future itself. The first thing I ask is the month and day of birth. It is always useful to know the astrological sign. That will give you an instant insight into their character. Fire sign? More than likely, if an Aries, the person is independent and impatient. Earth sign? Probably creative but somewhat stubborn if a Taurus. Air sign? Geminis can certainly be the devil and the devil's advocate concurrently. Water sign? Don't ever come between a Cancer and the family.

The other piece of information needed is the day of birth and the following descriptions of the Drom Ek Romani and tarot cards will give you an idea of what to expect for each number. As stated previously, it is not necessary to learn an entire numerology system. Read, study, practice and look at the person you will advise, listen to that person. Know that person even if you have just met. And become that person while showing empathy and tolerance.

I was once between jobs and needed money so I got a job as a phone psychic. The supervisors are able to monitor the "psychics" and callers. Disclaimer: I have never claimed to be a psychic. I am sensitive. Clairsentient. I can feel another's emotions. I am able to see manifestations of the dead, but only family and friends. I have quite often known ahead of time if someone will die. I still don't consider myself psychic though.

So back to the phone psychic fiasco. My first real customer (the first call I took was an employee testing me, although I wasn't supposed to know that) didn't ask me a question, she just said to tell her what I saw in the cards. I saw a confused young woman but with lots of potential. I was suggesting that she return to school when she interrupted me and said, "I just want to know if the baby I'm carrying is my boyfriend's or my husband's who is in prison." I didn't know. I told her I didn't know. Then I went on to suggest ways to take care of her future with education and she kept interrupting me and in desperation asked me to please tell her who the father was. Her tone of voice, when she asked if it was her boyfriend sounded so much stronger than the husband whom she obviously disdained. So I said that yes, it was the boyfriend. When she hung up my

17

supervisor was listening and she said I was doing good and don't worry about suggesting education and potential careers. I told her I wanted to quit. I said I downright lied to the caller and that was not how I viewed reading cards. I said I worked best with people who wanted serious answers about their future. I still remember what she said: "Please don't quit! These people are trolls! Just tell them what they want to know." I stayed on the rest of the night but quit by phone the next day. I didn't even ask for my salary.

It's not that she was wrong, although calling someone "troll" shocked me at the time. Now, one only has to watch a reality show or write a book and look at what "troll" reviewers say, to understand that the word "troll" is often mild. It's not that I was better than the caller or the other psychics. It just went against my code of healing: harm no one. A *drabarni* is a healer, not necessarily born one, but when undertaking advising for people in need, she should have a code of ethics to follow. In the above case I felt there was nothing I could offer that would help the questioner and although I felt compassion, it seemed more beneficial for her to talk to a psychic who might be able to genuinely answer the question.

I use the pronoun "she" for *drabarni* because both of my family *kumpanias* were gender-specific. The men were the protectors and the women, although they worked outside the home, were the healers. We women became vegetarians after marriage so that the men and children could eat the meat. Yes, as a Baby Boomer feminist it made me grit my teeth at times but I understood the economics of feeding our children first, always, and then the men who needed the physical strength. We are in modern times and I am still a vegetarian, I nevertheless make sure that all members of my family—including my dogs--have the last of the eggs or anything else (except chocolate, my favorite vegetable). But there are many fine male herbalists, healers and advisors and many fine females who could protect and defend a family or a full *kumpania*. The modernization of life alters much that preceded the present day. Like life, we must not predict with cards because everything changes, including attitudes and fortunes. We need only speak about the potentials of certain actions.

"Fake it until it's real"--Anonymous?
Not as terrible as it seems. When actions seem alien, as do certain thought processes, but are beneficial, pretend to think that way until it etches a path through your brain and becomes part of your healthy mental outlook.

DROM EK ROMANI
(The Path of One Gypsy)

In a small row home, in 1956 South Philly, down in a dirt floor cellar, a drabarni grandmother picks up pieces of wood chips discarded on her husband's worktable. Using a carpenter's pencil she sketches a circle with spokes and hands it to her eight-year-old granddaughter. "Ashok Chakra, Wheel of Origin," she says. "This is the first step on your path. One day there will be twenty-two of them..."

1- ASHOK CHAKRA

Wheel of Origin
A new beginning, no matter our age,
But origins always interfere.
Double helix: eyes, hair, memories...

1 ASHOK CHAKRA: Wheel of Origin. While designing this card it began as the chakra that is the symbol on the flag of India. Roma— Gypsies—are believed to be from one of the castes of India (based on the similarities of Romanes to Sanskrit). We have adopted the Ashok Chakra as our own symbol in the form of a wagon or *vurdon* wheel. Result: it looked like the skeleton of a Ferris Wheel. But in the way of synchronicity I realized that my grandfather worked in the circus. And so my maternal origin derived from a carnival or circus wheel, making the symbolism correct. That is why it is so important to draw your own cards! I added the horizontal octonary, or figure eight, to signify regeneration, and the little "V" birds to symbolize freedom.

INTERPRETATION: You have the power to make things happen. Your life is ahead of you, no matter how old you are. This is the beginning of a new venture. The past no longer matters, accept it as part of your training and enjoy the future. No one's life is without ups and downs so remember, the low times will not last, all things change. This is a good time to reinvent yourself if you have been dissatisfied with certain aspects of your personality.

The number ONE symbolizes beginnings. Whether we are comparing it to Joseph Campbell's Hero's Journey or the beginning of arcane study—the tarot's Magician--or coming out of the womb, it is a threshold crossing into a new world. This number does not represent loneliness. It is the beginning of an unpredictable but adventurous time with the added bonus of maintaining an admirable self-confidence and a strong family feeling.

How does this differ from the tarot and how is this similar? The interpretation of the The Magician, according to my own understanding, depicts the new adept. The hands are pointing, like some of Da Vinci's people in his paintings, to symbolize "As above, so below." The table with all the necessary elements: wand, sword, cup and pentacle reminds us of the secret of life—balance. If we balance the elements in our daily existence, we will have performed magic. That feat, and the realization that one can leap the chasm into a new reality by crossing the threshold into the unknown, begins our journey.

2- PHURI DAI

She With Knowledge
That is free
Along the space-time continuum
Why does wisdom seem to be doled out during the course of our lives?
Why cannot we receive it all at once, preferably when young?
The answers are all there
Within the Akhashic Library locked in our souls
Waiting to be accessed
Be sure that your library card has not expired...

2 PHURI DAI: She With Knowledge. This is the valued wise woman (grandmother) who travels with the *kumpania* or group. I used a serpent, the symbol of wisdom in most cultures, at the top of our world, looking out toward the universe. Whenever I look at this card I think of John Lennon's song "Across the Universe": "Jai guru deva Om...nothing's gonna change my world..." Well, we know that everything seems to change but the universe is eternal. As long as we don't blow it up by the use of nuclear weapons, it will be, just be. My maternal *phuri dai* (Romani, with a little European blood injected during slavery) believed that we must be careful what we say because there is an exact moment every day that a statement can come true. If you cried in devastation, say, at the age of eighteen, and if the technology to go back in time exists when you are thirty, will we find that eighteen-year-old screaming through the infinite along the space-time continuum?

25

INTERPRETATION: You have access to the Akhashic Records, we all do. This is a record of all that was, is, will be. The "will be" is mutable and can be changed depending on the path you choose. Knowledge is free. Go inside yourself and you will find it because once you are inside, you are able to observe the space/time continuum and instinctively know what is correct. If you feel too inexperienced, the adage "when a teacher is needed, one will appear" will occur. Sometimes a teacher is someone you least expect: an infant or a pet can teach you. Pay attention!

The number TWO further stresses balance: two eyes to see the world, two hands to help ourselves and others. It is also the beginning of the dance, one that requires two. For every action there is a reaction. It is *dharma*, correct behavior, that enables the universe to continue, that ensures society will stay glued together. Two is very self-protective but will extend to those in need. We all have the wise woman inside us, male and female alike. We instinctively know what is right. Listen...

This is so similar to tarot card number 2 The High Priestess. She sits between the yin and yang pillars with moons and scrolls depicting knowledge. In tarot, by medieval times, knowledge was external. To the Roma, knowledge is internal, we all know it, we just need to allow ourselves to unlock it. Whether part of our inner core, or something learned, both the *Drom* and tarot recognize the need to secure this balance by correct behavior.

3 – DRABARNI

Asked to heal someone...mentally or physically

Heal oneself first

Drab means herb but also advisor

Herbs, tea leaves, cards and candles

Elemental glimpses into possible truths...

3 DRABARNI: She Who Heals. My maternal phuri dai was a physical healer. Not a romanticized wise woman, but an earthy, flirtatious woman with a wonderful talent and a desire to help others. She related how the village people would come to her parents for curative herbs. Once, as a young girl in Canada, she sewed on a man's almost-severed fingers. When my father couldn't get rid of a wart after months of doctors and medicine (he felt we were American and had to act like Americans, so we used "real" doctors), she put some herbs on the wart, tied a string around it, mumbled an incantation and buried the string in the ground. Yes, it disappeared forever. I have no hands-on physical healing abilities but have a knack for making good herbal remedies. I also try to heal people emotionally by being a good and sympathetic listener. "Drab" means herb but a *Drabarni* is also one who foretells the future. I don't like the word "fortuneteller." I take this gift seriously and think of myself as an advisor. Please have respect for the cards and the people for whom you may be called upon to interpret.

INTERPRETATION: If you are not asked to heal someone, you may need to heal yourself. Pay attention to your needs and do what must be done. Are you working too hard? Giving too much of yourself? We must help ourselves before we can help others. Onions and garlic are herbs. Research their benefits in your diet. Nutrition is the best medicine. Ayurveda—the science of life—has many healthy recipes. Consider purchasing a juice extractor. Use carrots, celery, and kale for a healthful drink. Thank the Earth for her gifts.

The number THREE is very special in spiritual and religious ideologies. A trinity exists for the *drabarni* also: heal the body with medicines, the mind with listening, and the soul with intuitive understanding. We who have chosen this path must always be sure to treat our own body with respect and think through all the potential dangers that can occur when helping others. I do not use reverse cards in the tarot because I believe that nothing is set in stone. Why scare someone with dire predictions when it is so easy to change the outcome? As is said, we have no control over our body dying, our genetics are stronger than our will, at times, so we have no choice in preventing certain diseases; and accidents happen no matter how careful we are. But other than acts of the universe, most problems can be reversed. Treat your seekers of knowledge with the utmost respect and never frighten anyone. Learn how to advise others to alter behavior but do not predict anything that can be a self-fulfilling prophecy. Many people born on the third day of the month are positive and giving.

This also ties in with tarot card number 3 The Empress. The ruler, the great mother, the healer. She appears as one with the elements, the mother of the Earth, and the *drabarni* is also expected to live in harmony with the earth in order to help others do the same.

EARTH

Invisible bars,
Chthonic seduction,
Stay, do not go away,
The Earth is safe and grounds me.
I grow, but
My skin, a rough plant,
Splinters as I try to move.
Some like it.
Others do not.
I am an other...

4 – ROM BARO

The Leader:

Confidence needed to make correct decisions

Especially when leading others along the path

Be the family peacemaker, initiate reconciliation

A voice screamed, "Fire!" in the crowded Life Theatre

Lead them all to safety…

4 ROM BARO: The Leader (of the *kumpania*). He not only mediates between the members, but is also the liaison between the Roma and others. The Rom Baro is responsible for the safety of all in his world.

INTERPRETATION: Have the confidence to make the correct decision. You have the intelligence, as well as the sensitivity, to lead yourself and others down the correct path. If you are called upon to be the peacemaker in the family or at your workplace, do not be surprised. A family reunion may be in the future, or a significant meeting with your supervisor. If you are feeling at odds with life right now, volunteer time to bring together people with other people or necessary resources. If you have recently argued with someone, take the initiative for reconciliation.

FOUR is such a fascinating number, at least to me. It has always been my favorite number and I'm not sure why. I was born in April, the fourth month, but do not believe I knew that when I was quite young. It looks like the astronomical and astrological symbol for Jupiter, a planet of luck and laughter, so maybe that is why I gravitate toward the visual number. Mars is the fourth planet from the sun and I am an Aries, ruled by Mars. But four has an earthy feel to it, and my astrological natal chart is sadly lacking in earth signs. Four resembles a house. We think of four as a square and although square was once a slang word for nerd, it also meant square shooter, dependable and honest; most born on the fourth day of a month fit that description.

The Emperor of tarot card 4 seems more grandiose, having an empire to rule, rather than a tribe of people to care for. We think of an Emperor or a King as someone who directs the lives of others and his subjects are there to care for his life. This is the complete opposite of what the Rom Baro's position entails. So how is this handled in interpreting the symbols when there is a gap in the semantics and thus the meaning of both titles? In today's world we might interpret both as a work supervisor or even a parent if we are underage. It is rare that we would be reading for a world—or tribal—leader, so we look at the context: When this symbol appears, we are able to adapt it to someone who will help or hinder us and we discover which way it is by the other symbols surrounding it. If we are being a minimalist and are only looking at the 4 elements and overall part (a "jiffy fortune" so to speak) then we may want to look at another card or disk or random number to get more of the story.

5 – MUDROSTI

Esoteric Wisdom

Aids in situational studying

No impulsiveness at this time

Conforming can move one through a crisis

But remember who you are and never lose yourself

We access all by thinking and meditating

Time to leave the cavern and use that knowledge…

5 MUDROSTI: (Esoteric) Wisdom. Nothing in the world or in our lives is more important than keeping an open mind and learning as much as possible. This picture depicts a cave with steps leading…where? The Akhashic Library? The great library in ancient Alexandria? One's own mind? Various symbols adorn the entranceway and the rainbow, or seven chakras, hovers over all.

INTERPRETATION: Now is the time to learn everything you can about a situation. Do not come to an impulsive decision. Study, think, meditate. You may have to conform in order to get through a crisis, but remember who you are and never lose yourself.

The number FIVE signifies freedom and change. So what does both Esoteric Wisdom and the tarot's Hierophant have to do with freedom, let alone change? Below, I write "conforming can move one through a crisis" and most lives are full of crises. So in those times it is best to maintain an open mind and listen to wiser souls. The trick is determining whether the ones giving the advice are definitely wiser than what we know we need or must do. How do we do that? I don't really know except to go inward. That's where *mudrosti*, or wisdom, becomes useful

The Hierophant—number 5 tarot card--certainly seems to know it all. The question is, are we the hierophant or do we listen to the hierophant? Something to meditate on when we have some time.

(If you feel frustrated by my not giving you an answer, remember that you are not being spoon-fed. The whole idea of figuring out a path for yourself and others is predicated upon the ability to think, dream, and live your symbols. If you err in your prediction, that is called learning through experience. Just try to remember what led you to an alternate meaning: something more to think about)

6- MANGEN PES

Love Each Other

At least try for tolerance

It only takes one to love

More fun if the object returns it

But is there proof that it is genuine?

One can only rely on one's own love…

6 MANGEN PES: Love each other. Words from Jessie Colin Young's song say it best: "Come on people now, smile on your brother, everybody get together, try to love one another right now." *Try* is the optimal word. I'm very concerned about a phenomenon that I call "Tribal Sociopathy." A sociopath, simplistically, is someone who thinks no one but him/herself feels pain. I notice that some groups—family, workplace, or religious— seem to think that they are special and shouldn't have to suffer, but it is all right for others to suffer. They demonize other people/groups, convinced that they deserve pain.

INTERPRETATION: Try to look at others if not with love, then with tolerance. See others as fellow human beings who suffer as you do. Life is difficult. Do not make it worse by spreading hatred and anger into the aethers. Even if you do nothing to help others, have kind thoughts. Avoid road rage and shopping cart wars in supermarkets! If you are questioning a love interest, good news: you will have a happy relationship if you do not play "mind games." Try to be as honest as possible.

SIX represents compassion and harmony as a rule, but we must be careful not to take our own charisma too seriously or indulge in chemicals that will encourage the use of charm in an insincere way. Six is always love. Six is the female. Six is Yin, All you need is love...

The tarot card The Lovers depicts a mildly sinister scenario. An angel hovers between the lovers but the intentions are not quite clear. Perhaps the angel is Conscience, reminding us about toleration. Love is an incredible morass of emotions, a forest of confusion, and lovers--as we know--don't always live happily ever after. So what is distilled from the burning of passion? Tolerance...

WATER

In between the violence of bolts and booms
Water, in its many forms
Cascades:
Gentle, Harsh, Heavy, Light
Sometimes in the sun and sometimes in the night.
The table rises
We garden with delight
But like the element
Our emotions leak out...

7 -SUADARSHAN CHAKRA

Wheel of Time

If the world is preordained, how true is the concept of free will?

Do our decisions not matter or is it like life:

The cycle of a year repeats itself but we make each one uniquely our own?

Are we our own parallel universe?

Western linear, Eastern circular

No matter, for we all look back to the good old days

But today IS the good old days. Tomorrow too

Life is our career

Position and the amount of our salary are our life support system, not our life…

7 SUADARSHAN CHAKRA: Wheel of Time. This symbol arises from Hindu cosmology. My father, who learned this from his mother, taught me this theory. It is very interesting and I strongly urge you to give it an in-depth examination since I am unable to address it thoroughly in this writing. This chakra concerns the World Cycle or Kalpa that is of 5,000 years duration and repeats itself identically after every 5,000 years. My father believed we are in the seventh cycle. That is, the world has been created, destroyed, and recreated for the seventh time and everything has been exact. Does this bring the concept of free will into play? Do our decisions not matter since everything may be preordained? Or is it like life? The cycle of a year repeats itself but we make it uniquely our own each day. Are we our own parallel universe? The symbol on the cards should be a swastika, but that will always be reminiscent of *O Baro Porrajmos* (The Devouring/Holocaust) where about one million Roma perished as well as six million Jews and various other "undesirables." But please read about this symbol as it was before being tainted by the Nazis. I have chosen the Kalpa, or World Genealogical Tree to replace it. And yes, the tree is upside down.

INTERPRETATION: Examine your goals. Are they feasible? Can you make them so? You are walking the great spiral path and need to take note of how your actions cause reactions. A major decision will be necessary. In Led Zeppelin's "Stairway to Heaven," Robert Plant writes, "Yes there are two paths you can go down but in the long run, there's still time to change the road you're on." About ten years later he states, in "Big Log," "There is no turning back, oh no." Age may dictate how we react to challenges, but this is the ultimate career card (or your most significant path of life) so take a chance as long as it will not be detrimental to you or anyone else.

SEVEN is an intellectual and mysterious number. There is a timelessness about seven. If you are a seven, life may have been quite enriching. I don't know how both of my families learned religion but I do know it was convoluted and confused by the time they shook the shock of slavery off their backs and left for *perdel paya* (across the waters, America) the different religions were entwined, including the remnant of the Hindu religion that continued in the diaspora. I remember arguing with my Dad, in a fun way, when he insisted that the Wheel of Time was in the Old Testament but my grandmother thought it was in the Vedas (although she didn't know the name, just the general idea that it was from their land of origin). I present it to you as I learned it: a wheel that went round and round, each time the Earth was destroyed and we started again, and amid that chaos was the world tree that is present in many world mythologies. I felt it was important to choose that symbol as a way station on my path but as you will see, it encompasses many parts of life including our careers.

The Chariot is card number 7 in the tarot. A rolling forward but with conflicting feelings. It underlines the question of how one's life will progress as we become independent adults and are just beginning to feel our inner power.

8 – MEDVED NA LANCU (Urso)

Bear on a chain

Plays along with those in power

Free

Because capable of exerting strength

If need be

Do we run and hide when life is impossible?

Or do we get the job done and then run and hide?

Yes…

8 URSO: The Bear. Some of the Roma, especially during slavery—robija—in Moldova (where my great-grandparents were slaves) were bear trainers. The bear is the perfect metaphor for the slaves. Chained, used for entertainment or hard work, they must always play along with those in power. However, the proof of continued existence is the strength of the Roma. It may be hidden but is there when needed. That is the vital element of survival.

INTERPRETATION: You have immense strength but in the situation you are questioning, it is wise to keep it hidden, whether it requires physical or mental power. Be adaptable or, as my father trained me, be accommodating. It is not enslavement. On the contrary, you are free because only you know the strength you are capable of exerting if need be.

The lemniscat or octonary over the bear symbolizes infinity. Remember and be proud: you are the result of one of a long line of the fittest survivors.

EIGHT is a special number. In the tarot card section below, I cover the karmic meaning of the number eight that will describe your specific path. You may not believe in karma, and that is fine, but you have thought quite often about life and at times have needed some help to move forward. Always ask, it is an important lesson.

The tarot card 8 is Strength and is similar to this one. It depicts a woman opening the mouth of a lion but it symbolizes strength of mind, not actual physical strength. There are theories about why the Golden Dawn reversed (8) Strength with (11) Justice and you can find impeccable research articles on these numbers and reversals. In the basics of many Romani, 8 is a karmic number whereby one whose birth is on the 8th, or whose date adds up to 8 (such as the 26th), is asking or at least needing, help. Usually a 4 (or one born on the 13th or 31st) is the one whose karma is to help, especially those born with an 8. Therefore, card 8 is looking for strength of mind, not justice, at this point on the path, so I feel that Strength is meant to precede justice. Take care of oneself and then worry about the world!

9 – KAPURI

Imprisonment

Ancient way to imprison

A curse or sickness into

Amber or other inanimates

End the sacrifice

Chip away at the amber-bound ant that enfolds the curse

It can no longer harm us

But must be returned to the earth...

9 KAPURI: Imprisonment. This does not really mean physical imprisonment. Sometimes we imprison ourselves, especially in our minds. It is good to be alone at times but avoid loneliness. E Kapuri is also an ancient way to imprison a curse or sickness into an insect or inanimate object to free a person from illness or *jakhalo* (evil eye).

INTERPRETATION: Seek company! The word "hermit" is an alien concept in Romanes. It is out of the question to not have family or friends, but if you feel that at the present moment you are alone and cannot take action to change this, seek professional help if needed. If you are just shy, join a gym, garage band, anything with interaction. It is the 21st century, so an internet chat room will qualify as taking action to meet people...

NINE is an incredible number as even a mathematician will tell you. Have you ever noticed in the 9 multiplication table that the numbers are reversed? 9 x 2 = 18 and 9 x 9 = 81 They go from 9, 18, 27, 36, 45 (it reverses now), 54, 63, 72, 81 & 90. For numerologists there is a further joy when we add the digits: 9 + 0 = 9, 1 + 8 = 9, 2 + 7 = 9, 3 + 6 = 9, 4 + 5 = 9 and the reverse is the same! All right, maybe you do not find it as exciting as I do (9 is Mars, my ruling planet) but the number 9 definitely resonates with the universe. Many cultures, including the Chinese, find it to be one of the most important numbers. Evidently, we Romani did too because it seems to be the point on our path where we have to shape our lives toward an acceptable happiness. If you are a nine, well, you probably know...

The differences between the tarot card The Hermit and E Kapuri are obvious: The Hermit is alone in order to think and bring enlightenment to the world while the Imprisoned one needs to seek the outside world and let it fill up the void left by being alone. At the same time, there is another level where one is cursed and the cure is to put the curse on an inanimate object that takes on the imprisonment of the sufferer. Once the void is full, once the seeker is no longer suffering, it is important to then withdraw and think about one's life: why was one cursed? Was one really cursed? Is there some way to end the loneliness, perhaps by helping others to navigate through life? Always seek the Hermit's way of life, even for a day, to recharge the energy that is diminished by others. Share your knowledge!

10 – SLOBOZIL PE MAYA

Freedom from illusion

See through Maya's veil

Caution needed before accepting what you see or hear

As truth

The curtain was opened many times

But now I see the uncluttered stage…

10 SLOBOZIL PE MAYA: Freedom from Illusion. None of us will ever truly get free of illusion. It takes years of yoga to be able to accomplish that. Maya is a veiling power but when we release the dormant spiritual energy—kundalini, the coiled serpent that rises from the base of the spine (the seat of security) all the way to the crown of the head (the seat of wisdom)—it enables us to begin to achieve the necessary consciousness for liberation from the ever-changing world of illusion.

INTERPRETATION: This card signifies the advisability of trying to see through Maya's veil. Don't accept what you see or hear as truth. Once again, it is important to go inward and think about a situation, whether you are trying to decide to continue dating a certain person, accepting a new job, or moving. This is a time for a dose of reality, as unwelcome as it may seem. In early Sanskrit, Maya was the goddess of magic, art, wisdom, and external power, so try to use the positive side of illusion.

TEN is the first of the two-digit numbers that can be added together to enhance one's lessons to be learned. I believe that people with two-digit birthdays have more to learn than the one-digit people. For instance, ten is also one. $10 = 1+0 = 1$. So when deciding what lessons to learn, Symbol number 1, Ashok Chakra (or the Magician in the tarot) is added to symbol number 10, Slobozil Pe Maya (or The Wheel of Fortune in the Tarot). TEN people are able to manipulate their environment but must not depend on external forces of encouragement.

The Wheel of Fortune is similar to Slobozil Pe Maya because fortune is merely a chimera, it is subjective and it never truly lasts. As we age, the ability to get out of bed and use the bathroom facilities, unassisted, can seem like the most fortunate gift in life. When young, meeting the right mate, having a high-powered position, earning lots of money or winning the lottery can be the definition of fortune. So both symbols tell the same story: see past the illusion for a fortunate life.

11 – CHACHIMOS

Truth

Pathway to a secret exchange of souls

A daily road for observing

Nature, nurture, buildings, relationships

Even if physically blind

Truth will help us see

The eyes...

11 CHACHIMOS: Truth. What a difference this card is from the western tarot card of Justice. That figure is depicted as justice being blind, but truth must have eyes open. To the Roma, the eye is a powerful part of the culture. I grew up exposed to the dangers of *jakhalo* or the evil eye. Perhaps this belief was part of the slave mentality, as well as the counteraction.

INTERPRETATION: One must not fall into a black-and-white interpretation of a situation. Study every nuance, see the touch of gray (as the Grateful Dead sing). Use all your senses to determine what is really occurring. Learn to study the eyes, they tell all. However, eye contact can sometimes be misunderstood so be aware of how you use it with strangers.

ELEVEN is spiritual, intuitive. Eleven is never added together as the number 2. Eleven signifies a search for truth, for justice and although this sounds like the beginning description of early TV Superman, the Eleven person probably has felt like an alien in a strange world at times. The challenge to find answers exists but not all Elevens are able to prolong a search, let alone understand.

Although the symbolism is different, the end result is the same: determine the truth and then be sure that the result is as fair as possible (not easy!).

12 – SAP

Snake

Sacrifice

Delayed gratification as we discover ideas within and without

Elemental practical wisdom imbued with

The gnarled bark of a lone tree

Harsh hail metamorphosing into rain

Destructive winds tossing rooftops and people equally

Raging fire scorching all in its path

That will learn you...

12 SAP: Snake. The Judeo-Christian cosmology interprets the serpent as a creature of evil but the serpent is also a symbol of wisdom in more ancient cultures. The double serpent is still used as a medical symbol: the caduceus.

INTERPRETATION: Practical wisdom. You may be called upon to sacrifice something, whether it is an idea, a plan, or anything that you were counting on. This is temporary and in the words of Mick Jagger, "You can't always get what you want...[but] you get what you need." Accept with good grace. Sometimes when we delay gratification, the rewards are so much better than what we expected. Consider this as a period of growth.

Most TWELVE people seem to have special hurdles to conquer in life. Perhaps like the misunderstood snake, the scapegoat for humanity's ills in some mythologies, twelves must learn and will not be released until they do. Being a double digit, they are also a 3 and can heal themselves and eventually others.

The Tree of Knowledge is a very common symbol. The tarot uses the Hanged Man or sacrifice. Some commentators say it represents Odin who, in Norse mythology, hung from a tree for 9 days to bring truth to humanity. Jesus hung from the cross as a sacrifice for humanity's sins. No matter the symbol, the idea is to wait, study, learn and pass the knowledge along.

13 – STANA

The Rock

A time to be still

And not attract attention

Absorb the heat like a crystal

In the Painted Desert...

13 STANA: The Rock. Rocks look dead, but if you've ever held a crystal or stone in your hand, quietly, you can feel their vibrations, the magnetic pull of the earth.

INTERPRETATION: Sometimes other cultures state it perfectly, and so I must quote from Lao Tzu's Tao Te Ching: "Pure and still, one can make things right everywhere under heaven." This is the end of a cycle; a time to be very still and not attract attention. Be alert and aware but take no action. You may choose another card if you need clarification.

One can write an almost infinite amount of words about the number Thirteen. Because the number reduces down to 4, a number that denotes service to others, the message seems to be: Change. If you have not come to terms with helping others, now is the time to see what can be done, quietly. There will be no reward of fame or fortune but perhaps a thirteen will feel the rightness of their path.

Oh, with what fear we looked at the RWS tarot card 13, Death. The Grim Reaper with people dying around him is a very scary image. When we are young we feel immortal and being reminded of our mortality is uncomfortable. But I always thought of it, essentially, as a card of transformation. The seeker is now more than halfway along the path and since none of us are perfect it is time for a change. The death of the old self perhaps but rarely does it predict actual death.

14 – MARA

The Sea

A sense of humor produces balance

Be the sea

Blending with sand

With an airy caress

Of sun or moon

Completing the balance…

14 MARA: The Sea. Traveling mostly inland, the Roma thought of water as being important for drinking, bathing, and cleaning. The prime place to camp was next to *o pirovo* (the stream). To me, the most perfect place of balance was always by the ocean. I spent a week in Atlantic City (pre-Casinoland) every year with my grandmother. Standing in the Atlantic Ocean the wild surf would wash up to the sand and the current would pull the sand out from under my feet. What dizzying fun! By the sea during a sunny day exists the perfect elemental balance: earth, air, fire, and water.

INTERPRETATION: Keep your balance, be temperate in all you do. Retain a sense of humor as the day progresses. It may be a time to give in as it is always wise to choose your fights carefully. Go with the flow…it is all right to be accepting and passive at times. This will enhance, not damage, your image!

The number FOURTEEN means seek the balance. It is the secret of life! When thoughts are spiralling out of control, bring yourself back to the center. 14 is also 5—esoteric wisdom—so be sure to meditate. It doesn't have to be a formal type of meditation with special breathing. Just sit quietly, where you can be alone, and let your mind wander until you are able to stop the clacking of the brain and r-e-l-a-x...

Number 14 in the tarot is Temperance. Like E Mara, it is a card of balance and the elements are represented: Earth, Water, Air and Fire.

15- Shambala

Temptation

Rebel

With an almost-uncontrollable power

Recognize this and use it wisely

"Drom" means "way"

All paths can diverge

Tread ever so carefully if you leave the main road...

15 SHAMBALA: Quietude. According to the Tibetan Lamas, this is the secret place of enlightenment in the mountains. Everything is perfect there including the inhabitants, even if they are servants.

INTERPRETATION: Temptation. Nothing is perfect. For the average person, Shangri-La does not exist. Unlike Maya that veils the truth, Shambala shows that we really do know the difference between right and wrong. You are considering a situation that is not ethically sound. Do not glorify vices whether they be cheating (a love partner or in business or in school), the overuse of drugs or alcohol, or other unclean habits. That rationalization will lead you to destruction. You have great power. Use it wisely and for the good of others as well as for yourself.

If you have ever read a book about Utopia or seen a Shangri-La type movie, you may notice that yes, all is perfect for the heroes of the book and the monks or ruling class, but someone is doing the cooking and cleaning. Selective Shambalese...FIFTEEN is a very dangerous number. I am a 15. It is the crossroads of one's path and so easy to get lost. Fortunately, 15 reduces to 6, Love, so we of that number must remember to love ourselves and choose the correct way.

Another frightening card in the tarot is The Devil. In the RWS deck it mirrors the Lovers in that this time they are chained to the devil who has replaced the angel. Temptation! Not a devil with a pitchfork in the afterlife. This is now. There is no road to Shambala (who put the sham in Shambala?) so be careful.

16 – KHER

House

Permanence is preferred

If improvements considered

The house and I are the same

Both vulnerable to lightning

Flashes differ:

Destructive or insightful?

16 KHER: The House. Where is my home? Like Dorothy in "The Wizard of Oz," I believe that there is no place like home but I cannot find it! My father spent the first ten years of his life in a mud-floored thatch-roofed hut, sleeping on a stove in Bessarabia, Moldova. He felt that as long as he had a roof over his head, life was good. Perhaps this is where I become more like my mother's family. Happiness is movement until the search for home ends. After desrobireja (abolition), my father's family remained in Moldova but my mother's family hopped into the *vurdon* and took off for *perdell paya* (literally, beyond the waters, or America). They continued to move around Philadelphia, though. I suppose it's genetic. In 13 years I lived in 12 different places!

INTERPRETATION: At this point in your life it is wise to move around but not necessarily in a physical sense. Permanence is fine if you improve upon it: change the way you do your job, try meeting some new friends, change some aspects of your residence, or perhaps change a love interest. If you are basically happy but feel some minor discontent, see what can be improved: paint the rooms, buy a better mattress, or discuss modifications of household chores with your mate. Underlying all this need for movement is the onset of knowledge. Your powers of insight are on the rise at this time.

SIXTEEN is a love of one's home yet, strangely, we may crave change. The house, in dreams, symbolizes our state of mind and the condition and type of house in a dream adds to the mystery. Do you dream of a farmhouse? It can mean you wish you lived in one but can also mean that you want to go back to a more natural life style. You don't have to be a tree-hugger, just see where you can add pots of plants or a garden. The lightning is striking to signal you to pay attention to your insightful ideas.

People tend to worry about the The Tower tarot card with lightning flashes and figures falling from windows. Yes, something at home may need to be changed. For some people, changing the furniture can be a catastrophe, so it is not as frightening as it seems.

AIR

Atmospheric gases for the unaware.
We breathe unconsciously,
We see nothing but clouds and colorful skies,
Or planetary lights in the dark
Like no other element, the invisible air
Is a leap of faith.

17 – VURDON

The Wagon

Rebel against the acquisition society!

Find free fun!

Hopes and dreams fulfilled

In unexpected ways

(although probably not a lottery win)

Travel by day

Bathe in the pointillistic night sky

Wish upon them, wishes come true

In some form…

17 VURDON: The Wagon. Yes, this is home, the traveling home. As a Romani I learned that there is usually safety in movement. For most of my life I have carried a backpack stuffed with underwear, toiletries, and important things much to the amusement of my friends and co-workers. Part of this was the "just in case" training I received from my matrilinear line. I knew my great-grandmother until I was eleven and she was waiting for the Czar to come and harm her. My grandmother was waiting for the Nazis and my mother for the communists. So "just in case" anyone came, it was best to be prepared to run.

INTERPRETATION: Safety in movement. Or maybe it is time for a vacation. Visit a friend, get in touch with the earth. Have a giveaway or yard sale (don't charge much money). Rebel against the acquisition society. Instead of spending money, do something for free like walking in a park. While you're there, collect some rocks, shells, sticks, or feathers. They are nature's gifts and would look great in a thrift store bowl or on your lawn or by your front steps. This is also a period when your hopes will be fulfilled but not necessarily in a material way. So if you expect to win the lottery, there's a chance that you will not! But you will win something more profitable in the long run.

SEVENTEEN, a love of life and a desire to travel. There is also a tendency toward good health. Seventeens, or those who choose the card, often work up to a well-paid position and are able to afford vacations and a comfortable lifestyle. Seventeen reduces to eight which calls for strength of mind, so anything good is honestly earned and enjoyed.

The tarot card The Star signifies hope with wishes and dreams coming true. But those are earned if the proper attitude and balance is fostered in one's life.

18 – SHON

The Moon

Controller of the tides, planting, our lives

Bathe in the light during this prelude to creativity

New to Full: blood flows, tides rise, energy!

Full to New: this too will pass...

18 SHON: The Moon. Unlike the classic tarot interpretation, the moon is a positive symbol. Controller of the tides, planting, our lives. Read the Farmer's Almanac or the Moon Sign Book and you will understand. Dieting? Begin exercising from new moon to full, and diet from full to new. Great results! Making herbal extracts? Keep in a jar (and shake every day) from new moon to full to get the most out of herbal properties. Tooth extraction and surgical procedures should be scheduled immediately before or after the new moon to avoid hemorrhaging.

INTERPRETATION: Be aware of the cycles of life. The moon is peaceful and serene. Go outside and bathe in the light. My mother always told me to "stop mooning about," but sometimes a little bit of melancholy is good for the soul. Close the TV and moon dream. This is a prelude to a creative time in your life.

EIGHTEEN produces sensitive people in all meanings of the word. They can feel what others are thinking and that can cause overly-emotional reactions, especially if the thoughts are directed at an eighteen. The zodiac sign Cancer may be ruled by the Moon and Water, but eighteens, no matter what sun sign, share many of the characteristics. Because being sensitive can sometimes hurt, it is understandable that this number would reduce to nine, Imprisonment. Resist!

The tarot card The Moon has quite a few negative aspects that signify brooding, loss of focus and a general feeling of mistrust. To the Roma, nothing was more welcome than the night and the light of the moon. When on the road, what can be better than resting after traveling all day? Washing, cooking, singing, dancing, loving, all under the moon. When in slavery, it was a time to finally stop enforced labor and appreciate the joy of being with family and friends. The Moon is tricky but open: learn the phases and appreciate all four of the monthly gifts.

19 – KHAM

The Sun

Success guaranteed

As long as you remain modest,

Ever-mindful of,

And grateful for

The solar gift

Exploding spots of health and strength

And magical "D"!

Why buy it in the bottle?

It's free…

19 KHAM: The Sun. Source of all life on our planet. This needs no description!

INTERPRETATION: Health, happiness, wishes come true. Success is guaranteed as long as you remain modest and remember to appreciate the beauty and warmth of the sun.

NINETEEN, a triple digit number: 19 = 10 = 1, meaning those with a nineteen day of birth have three lessons to work on. The fortunate number, nineteen, representing the sun, is a true gift: strength, health, happiness, prosperity. Use it wisely, don't let it dazzle you, strip away the self-illusion, remember where you come from, and there is a potential for a seamlessly happy life!

The tarot card The Sun is, of course, the same as Kham.

FIRE

I want to touch fire.
I can touch earth, dirt.
I can touch water.
I can touch air.
Why can't I touch fire?
Use a symbol, I am told.
Like flint? Alchemical sulfur?
Might as well use a Zippo lighter.
That would be like using a garden hose to symbolize water.
How do I touch fire
Without losing something of myself?

20- GUGA

The Boogie Man--

Face fears

Something that has been hidden

Will soon be made clear

I looked in the mirror and saw me…

20 GUGA: The Boogie Man. The one that hid under our bed or in our closets when we were young. There always seemed to be a nasty neighbor or crazy uncle who threatened this menace. We're older now so drag it out of the dark and you will see that it is really not so scary.

INTERPRETATION: Face your fears. Something that has been hidden will soon be made clear in a way that will bring you great relief.

TWENTY signifies the willingness to face life. The number shares the wisdom of number two. Know that life is what it is and can be met with confidence and, yes, fun.

Judgment tarot card is an awakening to a new way of thinking in your life. Similar to E Guga, one of the secrets of life is suddenly, obviously, sparklingly clear. Arise and meet the day, you are now on your way to knowing...

21- DESROBIREJA

Abolition (of slavery)

Three strides across Earth and Heaven

Found a new home

Problem resolved

Familiarity breeds contentment...

21 DESROBIREJA: Abolition (of slavery). Life is sometimes a form of slavery. Many of us have to spend most of our days with strangers doing work we may not enjoy. There are many wheels that we are attached to: the wheel of life, the daily wheel (daily grind). How do we get free? I used a vimana symbol because in ancient Sanskrit and other texts, flying machines coming to Earth, and leaving it, are depicted. This is the origin of not only the Roma but of Hindus, Buddhists, and other religions. Vimana literally means "He who is able to take three strides across Earth and Heaven."

INTERPRETATION: Completion. End of a cycle. New life. Resolution of a problem.

Like the striding Vimana, TWENTY-ONE enables us to face any problem and resolve it if we are willing to do the hard work. Most are willing. Reducing down to Three, one of the industrious numbers—besides being spiritual—Twenty-one is also a grassroots person, interested in helping whoever needs assistance.

The tarot card The World, with the central figure surrounded by the symbols for the Fixed signs of the zodiac (Aquarius, Taurus, Leo and Scorpio) remind us of the four elements, thus all is in balance, all is right with the world. Although this card is the last numbered one because The Fool is a zero and can be placed first or last, I feel it is different than the Drom Ek Romani. The end is never the end...

22 – TATAGHI

Father of Fire

An endless cycle

Time to relax and enjoy life

I am my own womb

Safe at last…

22 TATAGHI: Father of Fire. What a beautiful beginning and end. Safe at last! My parents used to tell me a bedtime story about a baby wrapped in leaves and sleeping on the moon, safe with father.

INTERPRETATION: The beginning or the end of a matter. The endless cycle. Exactly where one should be in life. You are walking the correct path. You are no longer worried about the mundane scenes of life. A birth or new life. Permit yourself to relax and enjoy life!

TWENTY TWO is the most powerful number and people born on the twenty second of any month have the power to accomplish almost anything in life. Their early life may be challenging but the potential for greatness is there. Sensitivity, illumination and balance are present. Be careful of negativity for that can grow as easily as positivity. Twenty two is never reduced.

With the tarot card zero, The Fool, we have come full circle from the Magician who is preparing to leap the chasm, cross the threshold, and live a balanced life. When we get to this point we experience freedom from the Earth's pull toward money and success; from Water's emotional outbursts of jealousy, hatred and possessive love; from Air's mind games and aloofness from others; and from Fire's out of control negligence of what is truly important in life. Now to maintain it...

BASIC CURATIVES (DRAB)

ANTIBIOTIC TINCTURE FOR COLDS AND FLU/VIRUS

Antibiotics are so over-prescribed. Worse, cows and chickens are loaded with antibiotics to keep them healthy and if you consume these animals, the medication is passed along to you. Then, when you are truly sick and need antibiotics, they may not be effective because you have built up an immunity to them.

Here's my cure for the common cold, flu, or virus...what is the difference between them anyway? Oh yes, organic and inorganic RNA stuff, I think! *Sastimos* (good health)!

At the first sign of throat discomfort or sneezing, I gargle with equal parts of peroxide and water and then take a fever reducer such as White Willow Bark (contains salicyclic acid like aspirin). I then use a tablespoon of honey with 10-15 peppercorns twice a day. Pepper is used to prevent malaria in some countries where it is prevalent and is good as a fever preventive. Honey, of course, is very healing. In addition, you may also add honey to lemon juice and a tablespoon of whiskey, if you are able to tolerate alcohol.

Now try to make this tincture. A "part" is approximately equal to a 1/2 ounce of dried herb.

Extraction is best begun when the moon is new and can be strained off when the moon is full. This is scientific, not magical. As you know from the tides, the moon has a stronger pull when it is new and will bring out the herbal properties. If you need to do it any other time, that's okay too. You can use fresh garlic and buy herbs that are already extracted.

If using fresh herbs, put them in a jar, cover with extracting medium, and

75

keep in a cool, dark place such as a closet. Be sure to shake the jar every day.

INGREDIENTS

- 2 fresh bulbs of garlic (the healthiest natural immune enhancer). Be sure to peel the skin off the cloves.
- 1 part nasturtium or Pau d'Arco as a lymph cleanser.
- 14 parts or half a large Mason jar of Echinacea root to stimulate the immune system. Add Golden Seal and/or Chaparral if you have it.

Extract in vodka, gin, or apple cider vinegar. Strain herbs. Adult dosage is 1-2 tablespoons 4 times a day.

MOUTH AND GUM PROBLEMS

Despite it not being a natural herb, my grandmother was a believer in Hydrogen Peroxide. Always dilute it with water (half and half) when using in the mouth. It is beneficial to rinse your mouth with the mixture at least once a month.

If you are experiencing gum or mouth pain, try this mixture with kitchen medicines:

In a cup, mix half a cup of apple cider vinegar with a tablespoon of cayenne pepper and rinse your mouth. I usually have some Golden Seal extract or Myrrh from the health food store and would add that also but it is not necessary. This will usually keep the pain down until you go to the dentist or doctor.

SPIDER "BITES"
(and bee and wasp stings)

It always amazes me when I hear that not only do people go to the ER when "bitten" by a Recluse spider, but that some people die. There is such a simple cure and it is mainly plantain. If you have read about herbs you will know that it is beneficial to use the herbs that grow locally. Plantain and Florida are the perfect match but this is not a hard and fast rule. I am unable to grow Chamomile here, yet it always relaxes me and relieves mild stomach discomfort.

I used to make a plantain salve with herbs and pure beeswax until the cost became prohibitive. I felt glad to find plantain salve (mixed with Blood Root) at some online stores. This is a magical salve for spider bites. Recluses have found me quite often, while sleeping, and I wake up in great pain. One time I had eight welts in a circle as if the venom came from all the spider's legs. I immediately slop on the plantain salve and the pain eases. Then I use more after my morning shower and in the evening. Within the first day the swelling is alleviated and the pain is now just a mild itch. Green salves (plantain as the major ingredient) and black salves (Blood Root as the major ingredient) were used so frequently by my grandmother and mother and instantly began the healing process.

(I must mention a disclaimer here again. To effect cures, one must be in touch with one's own body. If you try an herbal cure and your body is not responding within 5 hours, please see a doctor.)

If you are like me and hate to use a needle for splinters, the plantain salve will do that for you also. If it is a very deep splinter I usually put a glob of the salve on the area and cover with a bandage. By the end of the day I am either able to use tweezers to pull it out or it has magically disappeared when I pull off the bandage.

SHINGLE PAIN RELIEF

A few years ago I woke up in excruciating pain and didn't realize it was shingles. Now there is a vaccine for it but either there wasn't one when I suffered from it or I just wasn't aware of it. Mine were on the right side of my scalp and partially down the right side of my forehead near my eye. The doctor gave me an antibiotic, some cream, and a heavy-duty pain killer but a few days later, after the contagion issue was over, I had to return to work but still had pain. I couldn't drive or work with a strong pain killer, so I made a paste out of aloe vera gel (I used the 99% pure in a pump bottle from the pharmacy) and added cayenne pepper to it. Instantaneous relief and it did not burn! Also, while home, I used apple cider vinegar, quite liberally, on my scalp. Yes, I smelled like a salad but the pain was relieved immediately. Just another gift for us from Nature.

77

OTHER HERBALISTS

Dogs are herbalists too. I have a large fenced-in yard with all sorts of grasses, herbs, vegetables and other plant matter growing wild. The yard is for the dogs to dig and splash in the little pool and to bond with nature. Anyone who has ever had a dog (and I believe cats do this too) has seen them eat grass and regurgitate it when they need to be cleansed.

My Chihuahua, JJ (for Janis Joplin), couldn't get the hang of toilet training although eventually she was able to remember to use a doggie pad. She was very sweet and loving but not the shiniest fang in the bunch. But when she was feeling ill that little dog would go into the yard and pick and choose certain grasses and weeds and would self-medicate as if she had a pharmaceutical degree.

My large breed dog, Max, had a fungal problem in his ears and paws. I had a medical problem which only Blood Root could cure. I bought ten plants—although it was foolish, they really were not meant to grow in Florida—and put the pots in different spots in the yard. One day Max came out, found each pot, and ate all ten of the plant roots. Blood Root is a fungicide and he knew what was needed for his problem!

It was interesting to watch the expressions on their faces as they searched and consumed the proper plants because of some code in their genes directing them. We can follow their example by trying to listen to what our body and mind is sometimes suggesting to us.

MORE ABOUT CAYENNE PEPPER
and my favorite herbs

If I could only include a few herbs in a bag I would choose cayenne pepper (living in Florida, I'm able to grow it year-round), apple cider vinegar, aloe, plantain and Blood Root. I have self-healed and prevented invasive cut and slash medical "procedures" with herbs but it is a conscious choice I made and then researched and put into practice. I would never advise anyone to do the same but would be glad to share my experiences through email, if you are interested. Feel free to friend me on Facebook and PM your questions.

O JAKHALO
(The Evil Eye)

In my path of divination called the *Drom Ek Romani,* one of the symbols is an eye called *Chachimos* or Truth. The underlying meaning is that we must search for the truth before we give blame to others who may look at us with envy or hate, and wish bad things on us. Yes, that does occur. Perhaps we sometimes get angry and do the same to others. Can angry thoughts cause harm? Despite Mr. Rogers singing "Scary, mad wishes never come true," I believe they can.

Many cultures believe in *o jakhalo.* The Arabs, Greeks, and Turks usually use the color blue to counteract it. My family (both Kalderash and Sinti) use the color red. I cannot speak for all *vitsa* (nations) of Romani, but believe that many also use the color red for protection.

Red is the lowest vibration of the color spectrum. It appears on the right side of a prism. The first chakra, the base chakra, is represented by red. It denotes physical security, the basis of safety where all other chakras can be built upon. Even in corporate businesses today, red is considered a power color and many women wear red "power" suits to important meetings. Red is also the color of Mars, the god of war, whose planet "rules" Aries.

Wear some red when you feel fearful or are going to be in the company of envious people.

In my family, a red ribbon was standard ammunition for *o jakhalo.* A small envelop containing a red ribbon and other talismans was kept under a baby's carriage mattress when the infant was taken out in the public eye. As children became older, a red ribbon was pinned on the inside of a shirt.

No need for anyone to see it. Sometimes, if I feel threatened, I *think* red for protection. The power of the mind is phenomenal!

Before I go any further, it is important to first figure out if anyone is casting *o jakhalo* on us. Sometimes we are just tired or fanciful. There is no sense becoming *turbato* (angry, crazy) over every little look we are given. Here are some checks and balances:

LUNAR PHASES: We have more energy from new moon to full, and less from full to new. Keep track of the moon phases. If you are unnaturally tired, it may be due to a simple ebb of the lunar force.

MERCURY RETROGRADE: Do you know about this three times a year occurrence? Usually in December, April and August, when the planet Mercury is observed, it appears to be revolving backwards. Ancient astrologers/astronomers felt that the forces of Mercury would then reverse themselves. Since Mercury rules movement and communications, things associated with these attributes would be affected. Next time it is Mercury Retrograde (consult the internet or an ephemeris), notice how out of balance things become: computers tend to crash, phone lines are problematic, people tend to argue and misunderstand each other, and worst of all, there are quite a few motor-related accidents. The ship Titanic, for instance, sank in April during Mercury Retrograde due to a miscommunication. Perhaps the planet affects the magnetic poles of the Earth at that time and this causes problems.

So if you are feeling that nothing is right during those months, please consider that almost everyone is going through tough times.

NUMEROLOGY: What day is your birthday? Mine is the 15th. Because I have knowledge of the tarot, and my own *Drom Ek Romani*, I am able to compare 15 to card 15 and interpret the weaknesses I tend toward. For instance, 15 is Temptation in the Tarot and *Shambala* in the *Drom Romani*. It means that I have a tendency to be tempted away from my path, to self-destruct if I do not control myself. Fortunately, I understood this at a young age and although my life has not turned out exactly as desired, I have managed to live an ethical life. It probably helps that $15 = 1 + 5 = 6$. This is *Mangen Pes* (Love Each Other). If your birthday is the 11th or 22nd, you may have very special karma. Never change 11 to $1 + 1$ or 22 to $2 + 2$. Eights and Fours may also find difficulty in life. Please see the beginning of this treatise for an explanation of the *Drom Ek Romani* and the individual cards. Or you may look into any tarot site to see what your special card represents. If your birthday is the 23rd to the 31st, you may add the digits $(2 + 3 = 5)$ and use that card. The 28th will equal two cards also (10 and 1) and 19 equals 3 (19 and 10 and 1).

If you have a tough life, it can be due to lessons needing to be learned, not a terrible curse.

SUPERSTITION: Sure, I'd be the first to admit it. My parents are descended from slaves. Perhaps this was the only way the Romani slaves could feel some control: use *o jakhalo* on those who stole their lives and freedom. Whatever the reason, it was so real that it was passed down to succeeding generations. So much is unexplained in the world. The power to curse is not really unusual and the power to prevent that curse, or remove it, is no different than the power of suggestion, accepted by most people.

NUTRITION: This is probably the most important key to our mental health. How is your blood sugar? Are you eating enough protein? My grandmother always grated raw carrots and squash into everything she cooked, even pancakes. Although she didn't know the words "beta carotene" she knew orange food was important for skin and hair. If you are not eating properly, you may tend to see negativity all around you. Please think about staying strong with a healthy diet.

A ROMANI PRAYER

After my morning shower I say, "I wrap myself in a golden circle of protection and only those whose intentions are good may enter." I envision this golden circle and, on days when I feel threatened, envision the color red during the day.

I then say the Romani prayer as taught by my grandmother:

Drago Deloro, man hai murra skepil o jakhalo. Nais tuke. (Dear God, protect me and mine from the evil eye. Thank you.)

I encourage you to create your own prayer or mantra or protective spell.

When my oldest son was suffering from teething, my grandmother taught me a chant to use while rubbing his gums with my left little finger. It sounded so esoteric! As previously stated, I now have access to Romanes dictionaries and all she was saying was:

"Little finger
Make the pain
Go away.
Son, be well!"

For most Roma, the simpler, the better…

Here's the prohibition, though: according to my grandmother, "only the one whose heart first beat under her mother's heart" could do protection spells and curing if the *drabarni's* child was in pain. That meant only the firstborn daughter. I'm firstborn so that worked well for me. My grandmother was not the oldest daughter and told me she felt frustrated at times since she was the only one, once they moved across the Canadian border to the US, who was interested in healing. With three daughters who went through the pain of infant cholic, teething, and other diseases, she had to depend on her oldest sister to murmur the spell or prayer and it wasn't always easy to convince her to do that. Seriously? Well, in my Libra Rising mode that forces me to demand a logical explanation, I would argue with her that it sounded more like a superstition rather than a proscription but my gran was adamant. So what is the cut-off date, I would ask. How old can a child in pain be before a not-firstborn *drabarni* can do a spell or prayer? My grandmother taught me healing the way she taught me to cook: "a bit of this," "a taste of that" instead of "cups" and "tablespoons" and she was just as vague on healing: "when they can tell you what is wrong with them" was her standard answer.

I previously mentioned talismans. My grandmother and mother used red ribbon. I love rocks and beads. Black rocks such as lava or hematite and red crystals such as ruby (very expensive) or bloodstone work well. I like beads and even though they are merely painted glass, they seem to have a lovely vibration. Glass is sand and thus earth. I have recently found eye beads and carry a few around on a red ribbon.

CURSES RETURN!

Please remember this. Learn about the *Suadarshan Chakra* or the Wheel of Time. It is very true that what is sent into the aethers will come back to you.

At times we all feel angry with others. Sometimes enraged! My favorite "curse" is:

Iril trivar tu dragosto!

This alarms those people who are being nasty to me when I mutter it. The words sound very frightening when accompanied by my flashing dark eyes! What does it mean? It means, "Back to you triple with kindness"!

Shouting the words—like a primal scream--dissipates the anger. There is no harm to myself or others. Please consider something similar.

Chakras and Kundalini

Moving upward seems to be a universal imperative. Kundalini, a serpent-like energy that Yogis believe is centered in the base of the spine, moves slowly, upwardly, along the power points or chakras of the body.

So Kundalini strives to move from the base instincts to emotions to power to love to creativity to psychism to wisdom.

Gravity is a powerful force to fight. Rising out of bed in the morning after a difficult day, standing up after sitting at a computer for hours, defying gravity. Imagine the force of kundalini trying to rise above base instincts. Uncoiling and moving upward, against gravity, trying to reach the chakra of wisdom. No wonder so many people tend to act uncivilized!

Fight that gravity!

EYE BEADS

I like to use 7 different color eye beads. Each one represents a chakra.

If you feel cursed in general, you may want to buy some beads (with or without "eyes") and use all of the beads at one time. You may want to sit somewhere quietly and hold them and feel the power that you can manifest. Ask for strength to fight *o jakhalo*. Visualize number 8, *Medved Na Lancu*, the Bear on the Chain or the number 8 tarot card Strength.

If you sense that there is a specific part of your life being affected, decide which bead you need, relating to the chakra. Here are the broad meanings of each color from the base to the head:

Red: The most powerful color for protection. This is our physical base and source of material well-being including home and family.

Orange: Represents our emotions. If you feel overly angry or jealous or weepy, your emotions may be tampered with. Be sure to have some orange on you. Love and hate are strong emotions and the cause of much jealousy on the part of others.

Yellow: A color of power that can be translated into a career. Live and breathe yellow to see if, perhaps, a jealous co-worker's thoughts can be counteracted in your job-related life.

Green: Having health or money problems? Green is the heart area. It is the gateway from the physical to the spiritual. Some consider this the seat of love, so if you are feeling cursed in love, use green or even pink to regain balance.

Turquoise: This will protect you if you are experiencing problems with friends or even creativity. It will help open your throat to say what you mean clearly.

Indigo: This is two-fold because it represents your third eye and psychic ability. It is also dangerous because someone may be harming you psychically. This may require more than beads and words. You must think and try to sense who is focusing negativity toward you.

Violet: To protect wisdom and spirituality. You will need to think in a lucid manner and be open to all sorts of messages and feelings when you are working on problems aimed at your higher self.

NEED EXTRA HELP?

Today's sources of DNA were considered mystical to the Roma. Consider: blood, urine, hair and saliva are used to counteract *o jakhalo*. These contain the essence of a person's being, the code that belongs to only that particular person. Pretty smart, our ancestors!

Earth: Hair (*bal*) can be used in several circumstances. My great-grandmother wore a small braid of her daughter's hair (my grandmother's) on her head. This can be for protecting a child, or binding someone to you. Maybe not always so good?

Water: Urine (*mutra*) is used for more serious problems, especially for infants. If a baby is feeling ill for no particular reason (listless, unusual sleep patterns) it is counteracted by using the child's diaper after urination. The infant's forehead, cheeks, nose and chin are gently touched with the *mutra* and a brief prayer is said to remove any evil curses.

Air: Saliva (*shungar*) is used to banish any accidental compliment. If someone compliments a person or especially the children, *shungar* is called upon. My great-grandmother, who died when I was eleven, spit three times on the floor (over her left shoulder). My grandmother and mother did an American type of counteraction. Say that we were shopping at the Italian market in South Philly and someone said, "What a beautiful child!" My mother and grandmother, in unison, would turn their heads to the left and mutter, "Pooh, pooh, pooh." Somewhat comical? Probably.

Fire: Blood (*rat*) is used in very severe circumstances. Menstrual blood is considered *mahrime* (unclean) as is anything below the waist. If you possess someone's blood, you control that person. Be sure to use it wisely. A person under control can be, at best, boring and at worst, dangerous...

As a caution, there are many different types of people out there and some of them like hurting others. It should be an automatic practice that when

90

you are with people you do not feel comfortable with, or when you are at work, if you must clip your nails, or clean out your comb or hairbrush, flush the clippings and hair in the toilet. It may seem strange to you but some people try to find power by using your DNA.

The scope of this booklet does not allow for further explanation. Please feel free to e-mail me with questions by friending me on Facebook (use either Clarissa Simmens or Clarissa Simmens, Poet).

One Conclusion

So this has been a partial sampling of one Gypsy's way of coping with the world while helping others too. As you can see, the everyday Roma and *drabarni* didn't really do anything earth-shattering. My father said that in Moldova, when sickness or other problems arose, his mother would visit the *chohovani* (witch) or the *vrajitoare in gaura* (witch in the hole) when only powerful *farmichi* (magic) could help. The *Drabarni* is the grass-roots practitioner in the scheme of magic. We know only to help and heal. We do not know, nor do we want to know, how to control others. I hope this treatise has helped you determine that the Roma are not stereotypes from movies and books. We are everyday people here to serve and you do not have to be a Gypsy to add your good thoughts and deeds to the aethers.

SAMPLE READING

Well, all right, I changed my mind. I will do a sample reading using the Random Number Generator method. I use www.random.org and select "integers":

It was one of those "oh woe is me" kind of days, where nothing turned out right. I felt irritable and not even a meditation, asking for balance from the four elements, helped. So I asked the random number generator for guidance and wrote down the top 5 numbers from the 5 columns. If any number was over 22, I reduced it down and these are the five: 12, 14, 15, 16 & 18 (remember, some of the numbers were like 97 that equals 16, etc.).

The first number is actually the "bottom" number, meaning Earth so here is the way it would look:

18/Shon (also 9/Kapuri) = overall summary

16/Kher (also 7/Suadarshan Chakra) = Fire/Spirituality

15/Shambala (also 6/Mangen Pes) = Air (Mentality)

14/Mara (also 5/Mudrosti) = Water (Emotions)

12/Sap (also 3/Drabarni) = Earth (Security)

I noted that they all reduced down to, or were selected as, double digit numbers. I sure did need a lot of help with my attitude that day.

I always start from Earth and work up to Spirituality. Here is how I read my general discontent and what to do about it.

"Nothing is going right today. I feel like a sacrifice, a door mat, unappreciated and unsure of my position in the family. I have some knowledge, though, and can't help wondering if I am allowing this to happen. Do I take care of myself or am I always trying to please others?"

"I feel so irritable and that's not like me. I want to feel calm and think

93

clearly but my emotions are getting the upper hand and I really feel like flinging around pottery and watching it crash against the wall. It would surely be to my benefit to take some time and think about the problems that are causing this. It is hard to get time alone so I'll go into the bathroom and turn on the water, a relaxing sound, and think. Better yet, I'll clean the bathroom!"

"The temptation is to argue and make others hear me roar but within a few hours—or even minutes—I will no longer be angry and then really can't take back those words. Oh, but it would feel so good to say them! But why argue? It really isn't important in the scheme of things. I care about my family and need to remember that. It is ok, though, to speak calmly about what I need and want too and then see where the compromise can fit."

"Our home should be a spiritual place, a haven of refuge from the deluge outside. I see that my reaction to the words of my family is a bit exaggerated. Once I calm down I can get my ideas across. Do I feel strongly enough to speak about this or is it just general irritation?"

"Overall, I realize that our lives are ruled by cycles: solar, lunar, holidays, work days, weekends. Most importantly, I need to remember that this is just one more cycle: irritation. Am I tired? Is my blood sugar whacko from eating too much chocolate? Cycles are in constant movement and nothing is permanent. Hmmmm, now that I've finished scrubbing the bathroom I think I'll eat a nice protein lunch and treat myself to an hour in bed reading that great murder mystery..."

A PERSONAL NUMEROLOGY MYSTERY

There are mysteries worthy of attention and then there are mysteries that loom large personally. Here's mine, but a mild one:

After naming my new dog Kali a year ago, I realized that all the pets I named over the years, beginning with the year 1964 (with the exception of my two soul mate dogs JJ for Janis Joplin and Steppenwolf for the Hermann Hesse book although I like the rock group Steppenwolf) all had a name starting with the letter T or the letter K!

Tabitha (dog), Tiki (dog), Tarot (dog), Kyaam (cat), Toto (dog), Karma (cat), Toonces (cat), Kali (dog).

I wonder why? So I've played around with the alphabetical placement and decided that the letter "T" is the 20th letter and the letter "K" is the 11th letter in the English alphabet. Looking at the Drom Ek Romani I come up with:

T = 20 (Guga) and 2 (Phuri Dai)
K = 11 (Chachimos)

So was my lifelong message that before I could find the truth I needed to face my fears and become truly wise? Am I making too much of a coincidence? Just a way of exposing my love of numbers, numerology and the mysteries of my place in the universe...

ENA DRAB FARMEKO (NINE-HERB CHARM)

Seems every culture has their Nine-Herb Charm
It is said that Odin hung upside down on Yggdrasil
For nine days to gain wisdom
He learned of the charm
And passed it along to the mortals.

The British have their Nine-Herb Charm
Etched on the Tenth Century Lacnunga
A manuscript that is reproduced online
They claim it works on snake venom
Citing Beowulf's fight with the dragon
Also known as a serpent
Although if the charm was used
It was far from a proof of its efficacy
Since Beowulf died.

We Romani claim to be the earliest users
Those who know me know I used to make a salve
In fancy tins
Giving them away as gifts
Somewhere along the line
As herbs gained in popularity
It became more cost effective
To buy ready-made from internet sources.
It contained almost all the same herbs as mine.

What a wonderfully spiritual experience
To prepare an herbal potion, salve, tizana, poultice
It is like cooking a healthy meal
For those we love
The Zen-like feeling of handling ingredients
Mixing them together
Greenery from the Earth
Water to cleanse the food
Fiery transmutation of chemical properties
Air to cool for eager lips.

Preparing the Nine-Herb Charm
Whether for snake bite, insect venoms
Or whatever has invaded the body
Is spiritual too
Three times we sing
A thanks for each herb

The final mixture is strained
Then added to melted beeswax
Cooled in tins or jars
And depending on the recipient
Sung three times as we gently
Place the mixture on needy skin.

ONE:

Ah, the one herb
Most secret and powerful of them all
Is Plantago lanceolata: Plantain
Plentiful and super strong
Used, by me, to get the Recluse spider's venom
Out of my body
Or painful wasp stings
Or even splinters
Best of all, boils and even basal skin cancer
Respond to the Green Goop
As it magically removes body offenses.

(Plantago, we ask you, in humbleness
To use your power and pain repress)

TWO:

Artemisia vulgaris—Mugwort—very European
A nervine that "cureth the shaking of the joynts"
That protects against diseases and misfortunes
Especially if used on St. John's Night
An emmenagogue for female flow

97

Encouraging the venom to vacate.

(Mugwort with double protection
Help us heal misfortune and infection)

THREE:

Nettle or Urtica dioica
Stinging plant of glasslike slivers
Inflammation reduction
Antihistamine
An additional herb to oust venom
Of one sort or another.

(Stinging nettle who brings pain
Remove the worst of this terrible bane)

FOUR:

Gentle Chamomile: krasulko (daisy)
In the language of the Romani
Matricaria recutita is anti-inflammatory
But also anti-bacterial, aiding sleep and
Removing stomach upset
(As Peter Rabbit's mother knew)

(Gentle krasulko, so full of healing
Return us to a healthy feeling)

FIVE:
Betony, *Stachys officinalis,* is protection
Against jakhalo, the evil eye
A cure-all for headaches and anxiety
But my phuri dai, Granma, replaced it with garlic
Unimpeachable Allium sativum or "siri" to us Romani
Hanging in garlands around the neck
Vampires? Dragons? Serpents?
Cut up and rubbed on the soles of the feet
Eat, eat, eat it with everything.

(Siri, powerful garlic, tasty and strong
An herb used for everything that is wrong)

SIX:

Thyme, or mushtin, Thymus vulgaris
Promotes perspiration in fever
Pain alleviation
And the ointment takes away hot swellings.

(Thyme, a delicious enhancer of food
Also an herb when we need to be renewed)

SEVEN:

Fennel, Foeniculum vulgare,
Wards off evil spirits and damages the "eye" of the adder (serpent)
Antispasmodic for respiratory passages, stomach and intestines.

(Fennel fights the poisonous snake
Our body is right when we finally awake)

EIGHT:

Crab Apple, phabaj in Romanes
Malus sylvestris in Latin
Makes a strong poultice
For inflammations and ridding the body of toxins.

(Phabaj, eat an apple each day
For prevention or healing, so the wise say)

NINE:

Cress is Nasturtium officinale but
Nasturtium flowers that we call dzuche
Are Tropaeolum majus

Or perfect for Florida: Nasturtium floridanum
With antimicrobial and antibiotic properties
Eat the full flower in salads.

(Nasturtium, lend us your power
Queen of the Earth, a healing flower)

NOTE: My Grandma only used several Romanes words for the Three-time chant. I do not remember the exact words but I do remember the idea and have reproduced them in English couplets.

SASTIMOS!
(good health!)